ROYAL
MUSEUMS
GREENWICH

# *Cutty Sark*
## Souvenir Guide

First published in 2022 by the National Maritime Museum, Park Row, Greenwich, London SE10 9NF. This edition published in 2023.

At the heart of the UNESCO World Heritage Site of Maritime Greenwich are the four world-class attractions of Royal Museums Greenwich – the National Maritime Museum, *Cutty Sark*, the Royal Observatory, and the Queen's House.

ISBN: 978-1-906367-98-5

Text © National Maritime Museum, Greenwich, London. Updated and expanded by Louise Macfarlane and Hannah Stockton, based on original text by Eric Kentley.

All images © National Maritime Museum, Greenwich, London with the exception of the following pages: p. 14 Robert Brettle; p. 19 © National Maritime Museum, Greenwich, London. Cutty Sark Collection; p. 22, p. 26 Eric Kentley; p. 24, p. 46 Brodie Collection, La Trobe Picture Collection, State Library of Victoria; p. 28 Photograph by unattributed studio. Tyrrell Collection, Powerhouse Collection; p. 31 (both) reproduced with the permission of HSBC Archives; p. 52 © Aberdeen City Council (James McBey); p. 56 reproduced with the permission of Mrs Ann Bryce/ Photo: © National Maritime Museum, Greenwich, London; p. 57 Tim Keeler

Designed by louiseturpindesign.co.uk
Printed and bound in the UK by Cambrian Printers Limited

10 9 8 7 6 5 4 3 2

This guidebook is updated periodically but please note that visitor information is liable to change.

# Contents

# Introduction

It is amazing that *Cutty Sark* has survived. After an eventful career spanning seven decades, by the mid-1920s it was the last of the late-19th-century tea clippers still afloat.

Built in Dumbarton, Scotland, in 1869, the ship has been a tea clipper; a wool clipper; a Portuguese general cargo carrier; a cadet training ship and a world-renowned visitor attraction. One of the most beautiful sailing ships and once the fastest of its time, its grace and speed secured a reputation that ensured its survival. In both 1922 and 1954, it was saved for the nation from the brink of collapse by members of the public. In 2007, a terrible fire delayed essential works. Donations from around the world and support from the Heritage Lottery Fund ensured the ship was saved, works completed and the ship opened once again for the enjoyment of visitors. Today, at the heart of the World Heritage Site of Maritime Greenwich, it is a national treasure – the last surviving tea clipper ship in the world with a story like no other.

◀ Cutty Sark's *hull*.

# History of Cutty Sark

## The China tea trade

*Cutty Sark* was built for one purpose – to bring tea from China to London quickly. Tea, produced exclusively in China until the mid-19th century, had been introduced to Europe by the Portuguese and Dutch. It reached England in the late 1650s and was made fashionable among the aristocracy by the Portuguese princess Catherine of Braganza, who married Charles II in 1662.

Despite being heavily taxed, tea quickly became popular among all social classes, thanks to an enormous smuggling industry. The East India

Company had been established in 1600 and awarded a monopoly on all trade in the East. Yet, more tea came into Britain through the Netherlands (illegally) than via the Company. In 1784, determined to support this monopoly on tea, the British Government slashed the duty levied on it from 112 per cent to 12.5 per cent. Suddenly tea was relatively inexpensive and it moved from being one of life's luxuries to one of its necessities. The Temperance Movement, which was particularly active in the 1840s and 50s, gave it a further boost by promoting tea as an alternative to alcohol. Tea imports boomed.

The East India Company had to pay for Chinese goods such as tea, silk and porcelain with silver. As there were very few Western-produced goods the Chinese wanted to buy, a trade 'imbalance' was established, which the Company decided was unsustainable. To redress this, the Company grew opium in India and sold it to smugglers to run into China. There, of course, it was paid for in silver. Opium had been banned by the Chinese authorities in 1799, but they could not halt the traffic. When, in 1839, the Chinese authorities seized and destroyed shipments of opium in Canton (Guangdong), this was taken as an affront to free trade and Britain declared war. The Chinese forces were no match for the British navy and China's defeat in the first Opium War resulted in the enforced surrender of Hong Kong and the opening up of a number of ports to trade, including Shanghai and Foochow (Fuzhou).

A second war from 1856 to 1860 resulted in even more ports being opened up to Europeans, including the important tea port of Hankow (Hankou), hundreds of miles up the Yangtze River.

Ironically, the East India Company saw little direct benefit, since in 1834 the free-trade movement forced the government to end the Company's monopoly. With demand for tea rocketing, there were, however, fortunes to be made for private ship-owners.

◀ *Unloading tea in the East India docks, 1867.*

▶ *An example of an ornate Chinese tea chest, 19th century.*

# The rise of the clippers

The term 'clipper' came into use in the USA in the early 19th century to describe the small schooners and brigs of Chesapeake Bay in the mid-Atlantic, which had eluded the British navy during the War of 1812. It simply meant a fast vessel – one which could 'go at a clip'. It was not until the 1830s that these were scaled-up into larger vessels, when shipbuilders began to rethink some of their assumptions about ship design. A number of ships that made very fast passages from China to New York were constructed during this time. Then, in 1849, came the discovery of gold in California. This led to a huge boom in shipbuilding – and a demand for large, fast vessels capable of tackling the awesome seas around Cape Horn, off the southern tip of Chile.

British shipbuilders may have been inspired by the American examples that began bringing tea to London in 1850, but they did not directly copy them. In Aberdeen, Alexander Hall & Sons had developed their own prototype for a new style of ship and they would go on to become the most prolific builder of clippers. This new type of vessel was characterised by a long narrow hull, a sharp bow (front), a yacht-like appearance, raking (angled) masts and a very, very large sail area.

British vessels tended to be smaller than their American counterparts. However, their hulls were planked with hardwoods from Britain's colonies, not soft pine, so they were less prone to damage. American competition in the tea trade did not last for long either: in 1857 the USA slid into a deep recession, leaving a huge amount of surplus shipping. British ship-owners were left to compete for trade supremacy largely among themselves.

▶ The tea clipper 'Thermopylae', *by F.I. Sorensen, 19th century. Launched in 1868,* Thermopylae *was one of the most successful tea clippers.*

THE FAMOUS TEA-CLIPPER
THERMOPYLAE.

## The tea races

For more than 150 years, the British had been content to buy tea with little concern about how long it had taken to reach them, but, suddenly, tea that had taken only three and a half months to arrive was available. The Victorians, with their relish for novelty, began to demand not just 'fresh' tea but the very first of a season's tea to arrive.

To secure the valuable first shipment, which could be sold at the highest price, tea merchants gave incentives to the ship-owners. From 1861 they also offered an additional premium of ten shillings per ton on the first tea delivered to London.

Competition among ships intensified and the legendary tea clipper races began. Of these, none was closer than the race of 1866. In May that year, five British ships left Foochow within hours of each other. Ninety-nine days and 15,000 miles later, Ariel reached the Kent coast ten minutes ahead of Taeping. But Taeping found a tug (a boat that would tow sailing ships up the difficult-to-navigate River Thames) and thus managed to unload its cargo first, and beat Ariel into second place by just 20 minutes.

The owners of the two ships realised that their cargoes, and those of the three ships yet to arrive, would flood the London market. They feared that the merchants would use any dispute about the result of the race as an excuse not to pay the premium. So they secretly agreed not to argue about whether the race was to the mouth of Thames, the dock or the quayside, but instead to split the bonus. Never again was the ten-shilling premium offered, but nothing could stop the rivalry among the ships for the season's fastest passage.

▼ The Great China Race: The Clipper Ships 'Taeping' and 'Ariel'
passing the Lizard on their homeward voyage from Foo-Chow-Foo,
6 September 1866, *by Thomas Goldsworth Dutton, 1866.*

# John Willis and his new ship

*Cutty Sark* was commissioned by John Willis, a Scotsman based in London, who had been a ship's master himself at 19 and brought his first tea cargo home in 1846. Seven years later he retired from the sea to concentrate on running the shipping business his father had established.

Willis had used a number of shipbuilders to create his fleet, but for his new ship he went to a company that had only been in operation for a year – Scott & Linton. Their premises were in the Woodyard at Dumbarton, Scotland, on the bank of the River Leven. William Dundas Scott-Moncrieff was the business manager and Hercules Linton the designer. Linton had served his apprenticeship in Aberdeen with Alexander Hall & Sons, the inventors of the distinctive hollow bow and the most prolific builders of wooden clippers. He was also an experienced ship surveyor, particularly of iron ships.

*Cutty Sark* was to be neither a wooden ship nor an iron ship, but one of composite construction. Wooden planks were bolted onto a wrought-iron framework and the result was both a very strong vessel and one in which the frame took up a very small area of the hull. This left more precious space for cargo. During the 1860s, composite construction overtook wooden construction as the principal method of building sailing ships for the China trade. In 1869, the year that *Cutty Sark* was built, 13 composite ships were constructed for the trade and not one of wood.

Apart from *Cutty Sark*, there are now only two surviving composite vessels – the passenger clipper *City of Adelaide* and the warship HMS *Gannet*.

▶ *John Willis (1817–99), owner of Cutty Sark.*

▼ *Cutty Sark on the stocks – a sketch by Hercules Linton, 1869.*

'Cutty Sark', by Frederick Tudgay, 1872.
This picture was commissioned by
the ship's owner, John Willis.

# Building *Cutty Sark*

Scott & Linton signed the agreement to build *Cutty Sark* on 28 January 1869. Willis was to pay £16,150 and the ship was to be finished by the end of July that year.

It was to have 138 iron frames, and a beam every fourth frame. Under the Main and 'Tween decks, a criss-cross pattern of metal tie-plates along both sides gave it the rigidity of an iron bridge. The strakes (planking) that ran along each side were of varying thicknesses. The thinner wood at the top was teak from the west coast of India, while the lower, thicker strakes were rock elm from North America, better suited than teak to constant immersion. More than 20,000 bolts secured the planks to the frames.

▲ *Hercules Linton (1837–1900), designer of* Cutty Sark.

The hull was sheathed up to the waterline with thin plates of Muntz metal (a brass-like metal consisting of 60 per cent copper and 40 per cent zinc, with a trace of iron). This stopped weeds and barnacles from attaching themselves to the hull and kept shipworm from boring through the wood, but at a fraction of the cost of using copper, the traditional solution.

However, delays in design led to problems with Scott & Linton's cash flow. The July deadline was missed and in the first week of September work in the yard was partially suspended. Work on the ship was taken over and completed by creditors, most prominent among them William Denny & Brothers.

*Cutty Sark* was launched with seemingly little fanfare on 22 November 1869. It was then towed to the Leven shipyard for masting and on to Greenock for the rigging that controlled the yards to be set up. It left Scotland on 13 January 1870. Just two weeks later it took on its first cargo in London's East India Docks.

▶ *Linton's drawing of* Cutty Sark's *(half) midship section, showing the elements of its composite construction, 1869.*

# N° 5

## Composite Ship. Under Special Survey.

Length 210 feet
Breadth 36 "
Depth 20.9 "
Tons. U.D.
2½"
SCOTT & LINTON,
SHIPBUILDERS
DUMBARTON.
Top of Floors
3½"


cale 3/8 Inch to a Foot

| | |
|---|---|
| Stem of East India Teak | 2.0" × 15½ |
| Stern Post " | 17" × 15½ |
| Keel of American Rock Elm | 17" × 15½" |
| Frames angle iron | 3¾" × 4½" × |
| Reverse frames | 3¼" × 3" × |
| Main Deck Beams Bulb iron | 9" × 9/16" |
| Lower " " " " | 10" × 11/16 |
| Main Deck Stringer | 30" × 11/16 |
| Lower " " | 22½" × 11/16 |
| Main Deck Tie | 13½" × 11/16 |
| Lower " " | 15" × 11/16 |
| Sheer strake | 35" × 7/8 |
| Foundation plate of Box Keelson | 18½" × 5/8 |
| Side plates of Box Keelson | 16" × 5/8 |
| Top " " " " | 10¾" × |
| Foundation plates angles | 3¾" × 4½ |
| Top plate " " | 3" × 3" × |
| Intercostal plate Keelson | 14" × 5/8 |
| " Keelson Bulb iron | 10" × 5/8 |
| " " angles | 5" × 4" × |
| Bilge Keelson Bulb iron | 10" × 11/16" |
| " " angle " | 5" × 4" × |
| " Stringer " " | 5" × 4" × |
| Main Deck Stringer angle iron | 5" × 4" × |
| Lower " " " " | 5" × 4" × |
| Floors | 24" × 9/16 |
| Main Deck Teak | 5" × 3½" |
| Lower " yellow pine | 6" × 3" |

Planking. Elm up to 8 feet 2 inches f
above that of Teak 6" inches tape

| | |
|---|---|
| Bilge Plate | 23½" × 7/8 |
| Keel " | 31" × 7/8 |

▼ *The ship today, viewed from Cutty Sark Gardens.*

# *Cutty Sark*'s tea voyages: 1870–77

On 15 February 1870, *Cutty Sark* left London with a general cargo bound for Shanghai. Eight months later it returned with nearly 600,000 kg of Chinese tea, enough to make more than 150 million cups. Even today, when tea is more commonly available, a cargo of this size would be worth more than £1 million. The records that would have told us exactly what types of tea were on board have been destroyed, but by the mid-19th century the British were greater consumers of black tea than green. 'Congou' was the generic name for good-quality black tea, but *Cutty Sark* may also have carried Lapsang Souchong, Bohea and Orange Pekoe. Popular green teas of the time were Gunpowder, Hyson and the now-forgotten Twankay.

The ship took 110 days to return to London from Shanghai. This was not outstanding and, in fact, it was never to match the times of the fastest tea clippers like *Thermopylae*, an Aberdeen-built composite clipper launched the year before *Cutty Sark*. Yet, these two ships made only one truly comparable voyage. Leaving Shanghai within minutes of each other on 17 June 1872, they kept pace until they reached the Indian Ocean. Picking up the brisk south-east trade winds, *Cutty Sark* raced on and by the time it was off the coast of South Africa, it was 400 miles ahead.

But then *Cutty Sark* ran into a heavy sea and its rudder came away. Amazingly, on a ship that could no longer be steered, the carpenter

▼ *The great tea port of Hankou.*

◀ *The jury rudder was lashed up during the 1872 passage from Shanghai to London. The figure at the stern (back of the ship) is the ship's carpenter, Henry Henderson.*

managed to fashion a new temporary (or jury) rudder. A makeshift forge was built on the Main Deck to hammer out the new rudder's ironwork. At one point the forge overturned, showering members of the crew with hot coals.

After five days, they succeeded in hanging the rudder, including securing the lowest fixing, which was 15 feet below the water. By this time *Thermopylae* was 500 miles ahead. *Cutty Sark* lost even more time in the South Atlantic thanks to running repairs to the jury rudder. *Thermopylae* reached London after 115 days at sea; *Cutty Sark* came in nine days later. However, it was the demonstration of seamanship by *Cutty Sark*'s captain and crew, rather than *Thermopylae*'s victory, that would be remembered.

## The 'Hell-ship' voyage

The crew on Cutty Sark seems to have been generally content with its officers. Most voyages passed without major incident, certainly in comparison to journeys made by some of the American clippers, dubbed the 'Hell-ships' because of their harsh masters and mates. The voyage Cutty Sark began in 1880 was an exception – it was indeed a 'Hell-ship' voyage.

It started uneventfully with a passage from London to Penarth in Wales, to load coal for Japan. On board were a tough and unpopular first mate, Sydney Smith, and an inexperienced Able Seaman called John Francis. Francis was a regular target of Smith's impatient rage and the two had several violent confrontations. Accounts from other crew members suggest that there may

▼ Cutty Sark at sea, taken by Captain Woodget from one of the ship's boats, 1888.

also have been a racist motive behind the antagonism. Francis, a Black man from Chicago, would not be cowed and during one altercation he rashly threatened Smith with one of the heavy wooden bars used to turn the capstan. Smith snatched the bar out of Francis's hand and struck him so hard on the head that he died the following evening. Smith was confined to his cabin until the ship reached Anjer, on the coast of Java. There, with the captain's connivance, he escaped on board an American ship. He changed his name but was recognised two years later in London, arrested and sentenced to seven years' hard labour for manslaughter.

The crew was outraged by the captain's complicity in Smith's escape and refused to work. James Smith Wallace, until then a mild and popular master, felt he had no option but to put four of them in irons. It was left to him, the second mate, the sailmaker, the carpenter, the cook and four apprentices to sail the ship. When the ship was then becalmed (windless conditions meant very slow progress) for three days, Wallace had time to think. He must have realised that he would, at the very least, have his master's certificate suspended for helping Smith. In the early hours of the fourth day, Wallace spoke to the helmsman, climbed onto the rail at the ship's stern and then stepped overboard to his death.

A Dutch pilot took Cutty Sark to Singapore where its coal cargo was unloaded and the new captain William Bruce joined the ship. He sailed it on to Calcutta where most of the crew were paid off, leaving only the apprentices and the carpenter. Cutty Sark remained in Calcutta for four months before a cargo and new crew members could be found. It then departed for Melbourne where Able Seaman William McGregor fell from the ship and drowned. The ship then sailed on to Shanghai, where the crew was granted a 'liberty day' on shore. This small act of mercy backfired when several men contracted cholera. The ship had to be placed in quarantine with a yellow flag raised. Able Seamen J. Hall, Michael McCarthy and Bernard Sullivan died in a Shanghai hospital. Next, the ship set sail for the Philippines before finally heading to the United States. On the way, Thomas Dunton, another able seaman, was knocked overboard and drowned.

To compound the misery, Bruce had not bothered to pick up sufficient provisions for the final leg of the voyage and had to beg for food from other ships. Seven hundred and six days after leaving London, Cutty Sark finally docked in New York, where John Willis dismissed Bruce and transferred the entire crew of Blackadder to Cutty Sark.

## The end of the tea trade for sailing ships

In 1870, *Cutty Sark* was one of 59 British sailing ships loading tea in China. In 1877, just nine were in operation. Tea was increasingly being loaded onto steamships rather than sailing ships.

From the early 1860s, steamships had competed with the clippers for tea cargoes but, possibly because so much of their hull space was devoted to coal bunkers, the sailing-ship owners did not view them as a serious threat to the trade. As the steamers' engines became more efficient, they began to make voyages as fast as the sailing clippers.

On 17 November 1869, five days before *Cutty Sark* was launched, the Suez Canal was opened. This extraordinary feat of engineering, linking the Mediterranean with the Red Sea, cut 3,300 miles off the journey from China to London and ten to twelve days off the voyage ... for a steamship. Unfortunately, the prevailing winds in the Red Sea are from the north-west and the complicated wind patterns of the Mediterranean make it impractical for sailing ships to use the Canal. Steamers, which could carry almost twice as much tea as a sailing clipper, were now able to reach London in 77 days.

In May 1878, *Cutty Sark* returned to Hankow (Hankou) but its captain was able to find only enough tea to fill half the hold. Despite twice checking in at Shanghai, all the tea had been taken by steamers. Only once more in its career did it carry a tea cargo – this time Indian tea – from Calcutta (Kolkata) to Melbourne in 1881. Instead, *Cutty Sark* was forced to carry a variety of cargoes around the world and it would carry on 'tramping' – travelling from port to port with whatever cargoes could be found – until 1883.

◀ *The Suez Canal – a shortcut for steamships.*

# The wool voyages: 1883–95

In 1883, John Willis decided to put *Cutty Sark* into the trade of bringing Australian wool to London, one in which a number of former tea clippers, including *Thermopylae*, were already working. The Australian industry, specialising in Merino wool, had been expanding rapidly since its foundation in the early 1800s and by 1870 it was the world's largest producer of wool. Ships usually left Britain in the summer and returned with their bales of wool from Newcastle or Sydney in New South Wales, or Brisbane, Queensland, for the London sales in the first few months of the new year.

On its very first voyage from Australia to London, *Cutty Sark* reached its home port in 84 days. It was the fastest passage made by any ship that year and it arrived 25 days or more ahead of the ships that had left about the same time. The following year, it did even better, returning in just 80 days.

So pleased was John Willis that he rewarded the captain with the command of a larger vessel, the Willis flagship, *The Tweed*. *Cutty Sark*'s new captain, Richard Woodget, was even more successful. Again and again he brought the ship back to London in times that neither *Thermopylae* nor any other sailing vessel could match, the best being 73 days from Sydney to London.

▼ Cutty Sark *advert for wool.*

Woodget not only improved on his predecessor's sailing times, but he also managed to 'screw' more bales of wool into the hold. He usually supervised the loading himself but, in 1894, possibly to teach him a lesson, the dockworkers in Sydney took matters into their own hands and screwed in over 5,000 bales – considerably more than Woodget had previously managed.

Despite the speedy passages and the amount of wool the ship was carrying, John Willis had felt for some time that *Cutty Sark* was not making the money it once had: freight charges were dropping and his little ship was facing increasing competition for wool cargoes from larger vessels. Willis began to cut back on its upkeep and its gear was constantly being carried away in high seas. Finally, in 1895, three months after its return from Australia, he decided to sell it.

▼ *Carting wool bales to Sydney, late 19th century.*

◀ Cutty Sark at Circular Quay, Sydney, c.1890.

# Other cargoes

Although famous for transporting tea and wool, *Cutty Sark* carried other cargoes. Leaving London for China or Sydney, it always had a general cargo in its hold, made up of a very large number of small packages. In 1872, for example, it departed for Shanghai carrying baking powder, cocoa, currants, fruits, liquorice, marmalade, sugar, tobacco, brandy, sherry, wine, hops, malt seeds, drugs, mercury and other chemicals, oils and paints, galvanised iron, shot-iron, iron sheets, timber, tin plates, plated ware, earthenware and glassware, anvils, spades, nails, bolts, paper, books, machinery, engine springs, pianos and other musical instruments, boots and shoes, candles and matches.

On the ship's last four voyages as a tea clipper, it sailed out via Sydney to pick up 1,000 tons of coal for Shanghai. *Cutty Sark* carried coal on many occasions in its career. In fact, in total it carried more coal than tea. Ironically, as steamships improved, the most economical way to deliver their coal to coal stations was often with speedy clippers such as *Cutty Sark*.

Tea and wool cargoes were light and would have made the ship unstable without significant ballast in the bottom of the hold. China could offer only stone ballast for the tea cargoes but, when returning with wool, *Cutty Sark* was ballasted with 200 tons of valuable chrome or nickel ore.

During its tramping period, the ship carried whatever cargo it could find. This might be scrap-iron destined for Shanghai, jute from the Philippines, deer horns and shark 'bones' from Australia or myrobolanes – a type of plum – from the Coromandel Coast of India.

Beer was also a common outward cargo, particularly for Australia. On its way down the Thames, *Cutty Sark* would also often stop at Gravesend to pick up gunpowder from the Kent mills, destined for the Australian gold and coal mines.

▶ *Advertisement for Cutty Sark.*

TO FOLLOW THE "WHITEADDER."

DIRECT FOR

# SHANGHAI,

The magnificent New Clyde-built Clipper,

# CUTTY-SARK, A I. 16 YEARS

(Owned by Messrs. JOHN WILLIS & SON,)

900 Tons Register,      G. MOODIE, Commander,

*(Late of the "LAUDERDALE.")*

Loading in the East India Docks.

This Vessel, just launched, is, from her fine lines, expected to prove one of the fastest afloat.

For Freight or Passage, apply to

# GELLATLY, HANKEY, SEWELL & CO.,

8, York Street, MANCHESTER; and

109, Leadenhall Street, LONDON, E.C.

▲ *Hong Kong harbour, looking west, c.1880. Cutty Sark called here in 1872 with a cargo of rice from Bangkok.*

▼ *The Bund at Shanghai, c.1880. Cutty Sark delivered a cargo of coal here several times.*

▼ The clipper 'Cutty Sark', by John Fraser,
early 20th century.

# Crewing *Cutty Sark*

When *Cutty Sark* left London in 1870 for its first China voyage it had 29 men on board – 17 able seamen, three ordinary seamen, a bosun, a sailmaker, a carpenter and his mate, the first and second mates, a steward (to look after the officers), a cook and the master. This was a typical sized crew for its tea-clipper years. However, in 1880, its masts and yards were cut down in size (losing its skysail and the stunsails) so that fewer men would be needed to handle it. In 1890, for example, it left London with just 23 men in total – of whom eight were seamen and nine were apprentices. Sailmakers, always on board on the early voyages, became less frequently engaged but there was always a carpenter.

Most of the seamen who sailed on *Cutty Sark* did so just once – approximately 650 individuals are recorded as having travelled on the ship during its 25 voyages under the British flag. They were engaged voyage by voyage, so as soon as they returned to London they were paid off and had to look for another ship. Many took the opportunity of a one-way passage to Australia. In 1876, for example, 12 of the 16 able seamen deserted. However, two men sailed on the ship on ten voyages – Captain Richard Woodget and James Robson, the cook – leaving only when Willis sold it.

▶ *Robert Kemp, First Mate, 1893–94.*

▶ ▶ *Captain Woodget (back row, wearing a Tam O'Shanter), his crew and guests on board in Sydney, 1887.*

The youngest of those on board were 14-year-old apprentices, the oldest 54-year-old able seamen. Most were British but Americans, Scandinavians and West Indians also signed on. There was even one man from China – the cook James Robson. He had reportedly been found as a baby, floating at sea in a basket off the coast of China, rescued and brought up in England.

*Cutty Sark* sailed in the world's most dangerous seas and often in storms, and yet in 25 years only five men were lost overboard.

◀ *Repairing a sail on* Cutty Sark's *Poop Deck, watched by the ship's boy, taken by Captain Woodget.*

▼ *James Robson, the cook (right), with Third Mate James Weston (left) and an unknown crew member, taken by Captain Woodget, c.1888.*

# The Masters

During its career under British colours, seven masters served on board *Cutty Sark*. The first was Scotsman George Moodie who had overseen the building of the ship and was captain for its first three voyages. When the rudder was lost in the famous 1872 race with the *Thermopylae*, however, he had such a furious argument with John Willis's brother Robert, who was on board and tried to force Moodie to head for the nearest port, that he resigned as soon as they reached London and went off to work on the steamers.

His replacement was Francis Moore, the shore superintendent for the Willis fleet. A Yorkshireman then aged 50 and effectively retired, he agreed to command *Cutty Sark* for

▲ *Captain George Moodie.*

a single voyage. The captaincy then passed to William Edward Tiptaft from east London. He was a cautious but successful sailor. However, in 1878, on his sixth voyage, he fell ill in Shanghai and died, aged just 35. James Smith Wallace from Aberdeen, the first mate, took over and proved to be a popular captain, an excellent seaman and a good driver of the ship. Unfortunately, his time coincided with the period when it was becoming increasingly difficult to secure tea cargoes. His third voyage – the 'Hell-ship' voyage – ended in his suicide in the South China Sea.

The next captain, William Bruce, was a heavy drinker, an unpopular commander and a poor captain. An attempt to blame the Second Mate for all the ship's troubles during the 'Hell-ship' voyage backfired and cost Bruce his certificate.

Bruce was replaced by Captain Frederick Moore of *Blackadder* (no relation to Francis Moore, the second captain). It was he who established

▶ *Icebergs
encountered on the
way to Cape Horn,
taken by Captain
Woodget, 1888.*

▼ *Captain
Woodget's dogs.*

*Cutty Sark* as the fastest sailing ship in the wool trade. His replacement,
Richard Woodget, was a brilliant captain too – *Cutty Sark*'s longest
serving and most successful. While on board, he also found time to breed
prizewinning collies (which were confined to the Poop Deck) and to learn
to ride a bicycle on the 'Tween Deck. Thanks to one of the apprentices,
a grandson of the famous portrait photographer J.J.E. Mayall, Woodget
became a keen photographer himself and left a unique record of the ship
and the iceberg-laden seas through which it sailed.

# The end of the clipper era

By 1895, only ten of the graceful clippers that had worked in the China trade were still afloat. The rest had been wrecked, foundered or condemned. They were not replaced – the next generation of ocean-going sailing ships were four-masted steel barques. They were much less elegant but had much larger carrying capacities. The sailing barques would continue in the Australian grain trade until the middle of the 20th century, but the fast clipper-ship days were over.

*Cutty Sark*'s great rival, *Thermopylae* left the wool trade in 1890 and was later acquired by the Portuguese Navy. In 1907, the ship was used for target practice and now lies sunk at the mouth of the River Tagus. Built the same year as *Cutty Sark*, the beached skeleton of the tea clipper *Ambassador* lies at Estancia San Gregorio in Chile, towed there after failing to round Cape Horn in 1895.

This was the same year that *Cutty Sark* was sold. John Willis, who would live for only another four years, had already disposed of most of his fleet and on 6 July 1895 *Cutty Sark* was bought by a mercantile clerk, John Richards. He owned it for just 16 days before selling it for £1,250 to the Lisbon-based company, Joaquim Antunes Ferreira & Co, who re-named it *Ferreira* (though apparently its new Portuguese crew called the ship 'Pequena Camisola', a direct translation of 'Cutty Sark').

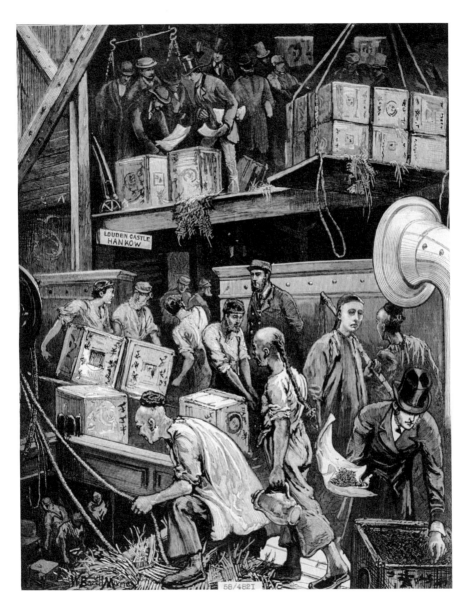

▲ The steamship Loudoun Castle *unloading tea in the London Docks, 1877.*

◀ *The Suez Canal in the 1880s.*

# Under the Portuguese flag

Before the First World War, *Ferreira* transported cargoes like cocoa and coal around the world in a vast triangle, sailing from Lisbon to Portugal's African colonies, then on to Brazil, Barbados or the southern ports of the United States before returning to Lisbon. It was in Pensacola, Florida, in 1906, when a severe hurricane struck. Considering that 5,000 homes were damaged and 134 people died, the ship was lucky to survive, although it was six months before it was seaworthy again.

It had an even luckier escape in May 1916. Sailing from Delagoa Bay in Mozambique to Mossamedes in Angola, it ran into a storm and its coal cargo began to shift to one side, making it dangerously unstable and difficult to sail. For nine days the storm raged. To save the ship, the captain had no choice but to order more and more of the masts and rigging to be cut away, until only part of the foremost mast remained. Finally, a passing steamer managed to tow *Ferreira* into South Africa's Table Bay.

Partly because of cost and partly because of the wartime shortage of timber, *Ferreira* was re-rigged not as a ship but as a barquentine – a vessel with a mixture of square and triangular sails. This needed a smaller crew but meant less canvas was spread, and so much of its speed was lost.

It was not until January 1918, nearly two years later, that *Ferreira* was fully repaired and ready to sail. It was sold later that year to another Portuguese ship-owner, João Pires Correia. In 1922, after calling at London, it put into Falmouth for two months with minor damage. In June that same year, it was sold again to Cia de Navegaçao de Portugal, Lisbon, who named it *Maria do Amparo* ('Mary that shelters', a reference to the Virgin Mary).

▶ Ferreira in
Limehouse,
London, 1921.

◀ Crew members
working on board
Ferreira.

◁ Ferreira near Table Bay, South Africa, with only its lower foremast remaining after a storm in 1916.

# Saved for the nation

While in Falmouth in 1922, *Ferreira* was spotted by a retired sea captain called Wilfred Dowman. Despite its battered and much-altered appearance, he recognised it as *Cutty Sark*, the same vessel that had surged past him in 1895 when he was a 16-year-old apprentice on board the sailing ship *Hawkdale*. He was determined to save it for the nation and pursued it back to Portugal.

It was Dowman's vision that saved *Cutty Sark*, but credit also belongs to his wife Catharine. She was a member of the wealthy Courtauld family, famous for its textile manufacturing, and so had far more resources than her husband. They were able to buy the ship for £3,500, very much more than its commercial value, and considerably more than the sale price 27 years earlier.

▲ *Between 1922 and 1938, Cutty Sark left Falmouth only once – to be the flagship at the Fowey Regatta in 1924.*

▲ *Cadets were taught more than seamanship skills on board* Cutty Sark *after it was purchased by Dowman in 1922.*

▶ Cutty Sark *in Falmouth, restored as a clipper ship.*

It was towed all the way from Portugal, reaching Falmouth on 2 October 1922. Re-registered as *Cutty Sark*, it was moored in Falmouth Harbour, off the foreshore of Trefussis Fields, Flushing, and Dowman set about restoring the clipper's original appearance. Dowman wanted *Cutty Sark* primarily as a sail-training ship, to train boys in the skills of seamanship. However, he also opened it as an attraction, with visitors arriving by rowing boat. This began shortly before the public could go on board HMS *Victory*, so *Cutty Sark* was the first historic ship to be open as an attraction since Sir Francis Drake's *Golden Hind* at Deptford in the 1580s.

# Back to the Thames

Wilfred Dowman died in 1936 leaving no one to take over the ship in Falmouth. Fortunately, the Incorporated Thames Nautical College at Greenhithe, on the River Thames, offered it a berth and Mrs Dowman presented the ship to the institution – along with a gift of £5,000 for its upkeep. In 1938 *Cutty Sark* made its last sea voyage, under tow, to its new home, alongside HMS *Worcester*, an old 86-gun warship.

The outbreak of the Second World War saw further changes to *Cutty Sark*'s masts and rigging, to reduce its size as a target for enemy bombers. It was also converted to an emergency shelter for the College's cadets. Its decks were made gas-proof, sandbags were filled with ballast from its hold, decontamination showers were installed, and boarding nets and ladders were placed over the sides for fast embarking and disembarking.

In the event, these preparations proved unnecessary. The government decided to evacuate all training ships and the College moved to Foots Cray Place in south-east London. Ironically, the new site suffered substantial bomb damage, while *Cutty Sark* survived the war unscathed.

Little regular maintenance was undertaken during those years, however, and by the end of the war the ship was in desperate need of a refit. But the College's priorities now lay elsewhere. In January 1946, it had taken possession of a new vessel from the Admiralty – the former HMS *Exmouth* – and the College's resources were ploughed into converting it into a modern training vessel. Neither sail training nor *Cutty Sark* was wanted.

▶ *Cadets on the ship at Greenhithe.*

# To Greenwich

It was at this point that Frank Carr, the Director of the National Maritime Museum, stepped forward as the third saviour of *Cutty Sark*. He persuaded the London County Council to make the site of the badly bomb-damaged Ship Hotel in Greenwich available for the clipper. He even convinced them to pay for it to be towed to Millwall Docks in February 1951 for a survey and a coat of paint before it was anchored off Deptford as part of the Festival of Britain. *Cutty Sark* stayed there until October to test public interest in a more permanent display of the ship.

Crucially, Carr had also engaged the support and enthusiasm of HRH Prince Philip, Duke of Edinburgh. This led to the establishment of the Cutty Sark Preservation Society, which succeeded in raising the £250,000 needed for the restoration from members of the public.

At high tide on 10 December 1954, *Cutty Sark* was floated into a purpose-built dock, still with less than half a metre between the keel and the concrete bottom. When the tide retreated, the dock emptied and the channel linking it to the River Thames was filled with earth.

The ship had been altered many times since 1869: for repairs, after accidents, for different crews and needs, and later to house and train cadets. After much research, the ship was returned to its 1872 appearance, just after the forward deckhouse had been added. A few minor compromises were made – the stairs into the captain's accommodation by the wheel, added by the Portuguese owners, were, for instance, kept to improve the route through the ship and to avoid removing material of historic significance.

◀ Cutty Sark *entering its Greenwich dock, 1954.*

# *Cutty Sark* as memorial

Part of the justification for saving *Cutty Sark* was the wish to preserve it as a permanent memorial to the Merchant Navy, and particularly those lost in the two World Wars.

The sculptor Maurice Lambert (1901–64) was commissioned to design a memorial wreath. Its accompanying plaques read:

*In memory of those whose service in the Merchant Navy helped to enlarge the livelihood of Britain and protect the freedom of the British Commonwealth of Nations.*

*Here to commemorate an era the Cutty Sark has been preserved as a tribute to the ships and men of the Merchant Navy in the days of sail.*

▲ 'Cutty Sark', East India Dock 13 September 1954, showing restoration of the deck, *by James McBey, who also designed the Cutty Sark whisky label.*

The second plaque ends with the couplet: 'They mark our passage as a race of men. Earth will not see such ships as these again.' These are the final lines of John Masefield's poem *Ships*, published in 1912.

# The 2006–12 conservation project

Opening to the public in 1957, *Cutty Sark* soon became one of London's most successful tourist attractions and more than 16 million visitors have since walked its decks. However, it soon became clear that the ship was showing its age. The sheathing was replaced in the 1960s and by the 1970s the iron framework was showing signs of weakness. A survey completed in the mid-1990s concluded that, without major efforts to conserve the iron and strengthen the hull structure, the ship would not last the decade. It was estimated that more than 60 per cent of the fastenings holding the planking to the frame had failed. Furthermore, the deck, which had been replaced and repaired often over the years, leaked badly. Worst of all, the shape of the hull – *Cutty Sark*'s most distinctive feature – was beginning to distort as the ship rested on its keel, or bottom, propped with supports. *Cutty Sark* was in need of major conservation.

▼ *The ship's counter is removed for conservation, April 2008.*

▲ *Conservation work continuing in April 2008.*

Recognising the ship's importance to the nation's maritime history, the Heritage Lottery Fund and a number of other supporters stepped forward, funding the plans to replace the leaking deck, remove all the planks to treat the ironwork and introduce a new support system. The aim was not to restore the ship to a seaworthy state, but to conserve it – that is, to ensure the long-term stability of as much of the ship's fabric from its working life as possible. Because of its composite construction of iron and wood – each requiring very different treatments – it was one of the most complex conservation projects ever undertaken on a historic ship.

In November 2006, the ship closed to the public and work began. Less than a year later, in the early hours of Monday 21 May 2007, a serious fire broke out. The London Fire Brigade very quickly brought the blaze under control. By great good fortune, a very large number of the hull planks and most of the furniture, fixtures and fittings had been

▲ *Queen Elizabeth II reopening Cutty Sark on 25 April 2012.*

removed for conservation. Some of the metal framework was distorted but no more than five per cent of the ship's original fabric was lost.

The fire delayed the project considerably, but work continued, and in spring 2011 one of the most important elements of the scheme took place: to relieve the keel of the weight of the ship. To preserve the unique shape – and to allow visitors to see its beautiful form properly – *Cutty Sark* was raised over three metres into the air.

Finally, *Cutty Sark* was re-opened by Queen Elizabeth II on 25 April 2012, almost 55 years after she had first performed this task.

▶ Cutty Sark *lifted*,
*by Tim Keeler, 2011.*

◀ Conserving the
'Cutty Sark', *by John
Bryce RE, 2008.*

# Enduring fame

*Cutty Sark* was already a celebrated ship when it was making its record-breaking runs back from Australia. During its long, enforced stay in Cape Town under the Portuguese flag its crew was happy to show this legendary clipper to curious visitors.

In March 1923, London wine merchants Berry Brothers & Rudd invited James McBey, a renowned Scottish artist, to lunch. The conversation turned to the company's plan to create its own blend of whisky for export to the American market as soon as Prohibition ended (although this would not, in fact, be for another ten years). But what to call the whisky? *Cutty Sark*'s recent return to Britain had been headline news and so 'Cutty Sark' was proposed as a memorable name. McBey sketched out a design for the label there and then – the clipper in full sail – and one of the world's most famous brands was born.

*Cutty Sark* inspired circumnavigator Sir Francis Chichester to recreate the Australian wool clippers' route in his boat, *Gipsy Moth IV*. Stephen Paine, future designer of the *Queen Mary II*, was similarly motivated by a childhood visit to take up naval architecture. It continues to be an inspiration to countless thousands of others; the subject of paintings and models alike.

When *Cutty Sark* caught fire in 2007, enquiries about the extent of the damage flooded in from all corners of the globe – a clear demonstration that it remains one of the most famous and best-loved ships in the world. This beautiful ship is the epitome of an era, the last authentic reminder of the great days of sail.

▶ *Medal depicting Sir Francis Chichester (1901–72). Designed by Paul Vincze, made by Spink & Son Ltd, 1966–67.*

▲ The 'Cutty Sark' and a Tug, *by John Everett, 1921. One of a number of pictures of the ship painted by Everett in the 1920s and 1930s.*

# Cutty Sark
# in focus

**NANNIE**

*Nannie is Cutty Sark's figurehead. She is based on the beautiful young witch from Robert Burns's poem Tam o' Shanter. In the poem, Tam is riding home on his faithful horse Maggie when, peering into a nearby church, he sees warlocks and witches dancing to a tune played by the Devil. The witches are all repulsive except for Nannie, cavorting in her cutty sark (a short underskirt or shift). In his excitement, Tam reveals he had been watching by exclaiming 'weel done, Cutty-sark!' and a wild chase ensues. He heads for a bridge, knowing witches cannot cross running water, but Nannie grabs Maggie's tail before horse and rider can escape. This Nannie, arm outstretched and holding a horse's tail, became the ship's figurehead. When in port, it was down to the apprentices to place a wad of unpicked rope in her hand to represent poor Maggie's tail. But why owner John Willis chose the name for his new ship is a mystery. Collisions, wear and tear have meant that the figurehead has been replaced several times. In 2021 Andy Peters carved the current Nannie using the original drawings for the design of Cutty Sark by Hercules Linton, which were discovered after the previous figurehead was carved.*

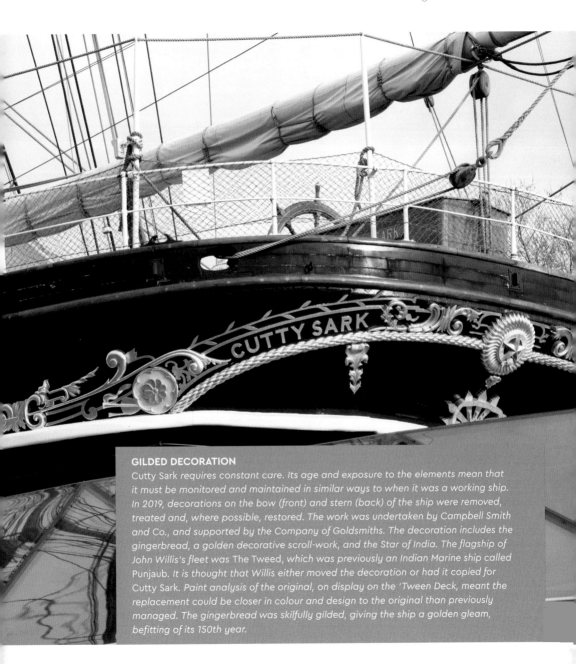

### GILDED DECORATION

*Cutty Sark requires constant care. Its age and exposure to the elements mean that it must be monitored and maintained in similar ways to when it was a working ship. In 2019, decorations on the bow (front) and stern (back) of the ship were removed, treated and, where possible, restored. The work was undertaken by Campbell Smith and Co., and supported by the Company of Goldsmiths. The decoration includes the gingerbread, a golden decorative scroll-work, and the Star of India. The flagship of John Willis's fleet was The Tweed, which was previously an Indian Marine ship called Punjaub. It is thought that Willis either moved the decoration or had it copied for Cutty Sark. Paint analysis of the original, on display on the 'Tween Deck, meant the replacement could be closer in colour and design to the original than previously managed. The gingerbread was skilfully gilded, giving the ship a golden gleam, befitting of its 150th year.*

**VIEW FROM THE BOW**

*If you stand at the bow of Cutty Sark today, you can see the Thames winding past the ship. Just across the river lies the area of London known as Docklands. While the area is now dominated by skyscrapers, in the 19th century it was at the centre of the Port of London, then among the busiest ports in the world. It was Cutty Sark's home port, the starting point from which the ship traversed the globe. In the early 1800s, huge dock complexes were built to cope with the volume of goods pouring into the capital from across the world. One of these, East India Dock, was where Cutty Sark's tea cargoes were unloaded. It is fitting that, in 1954, the ship was given a permanent spot overlooking the river on which it had spent much of its working life, reminiscent of a time when the Thames was filled with ships just like Cutty Sark.*

## COMPOSITE CONSTRUCTION

Cutty Sark's *fine lines, raking masts and composite construction are considered the pinnacle of clipper ship design. Composite construction combined wood and iron to great effect. A wrought iron frame was fastened to hull planks of east Indian teak and American rock elm. This resulted in a very strong vessel but also one in which the frame took up a very small area of the hull, compared to the massive beams a wooden ship needed. This left more precious space for cargo. The hull was sheathed with Muntz or 'yellow metal', a brass alloy devised by Frederick Muntz. It provided an effective and affordable way of protecting ships from woodworm and fouling. George Moodie, the ship's first master recalled: 'I never sailed a finer ship. At 10 or 12 knots an hour she did not disturb the water at all. She was the fastest ship of her day, a grand ship, and a ship that will last for ever.'*

XXII
XXI
XX
XIX
XVIII
XVII
XVI
XV
XIV
XIII
XII
XI
X

### THE HULL

Cutty Sark's hull was designed to maximise speed through the water without sacrificing precious cargo space. The shape of the hull is extremely narrow, especially when compared with other cargo vessels of the time, and it has a sharp-angled bow, allowing the ship to cut through the water smoothly. The hull's distinctive golden colour is created by its Muntz metal sheathing. The damage caused by shipworm and the drag of barnacles and weed was first solved by covering hulls in copper sheets. The metal reacted with the seawater and prevented creatures latching on. However, copper was expensive, so cheaper alloys like Muntz were developed instead.

## BUCKLING OF IRON

The fabric of Cutty Sark reveals much about its history, but not just its life at sea. In the ship's Lower Hold, iron plates beneath the deck above were warped by a fire in May 2007, during which temperatures reached 1,000°C. The London Fire Brigade responded quickly but the blaze raged through all three decks. Images of the historic ship alight spread across the globe and many believed it had been destroyed. In fact, the ship had closed in 2006 for an extensive restoration project and much of the fabric from 1869 had already been stripped for treatment. The fire made the project more costly, complex and lengthy, but very little of the original material was destroyed. The buckled metal is now a symbol of Cutty Sark's lucky escape.

## HISTORIC AND MODERN STRUCTURE

Cutty Sark was brought to Greenwich in 1954 and berthed in a specially built dry dock, as it was felt that it would not survive if kept in water. It was supported only by props. A survey in the 1990s revealed that, after 40 years, the structure was so weak that it might not endure another decade. Something drastic had to be done and, with support from the Heritage Lottery Fund and other generous donations, the 2006 restoration project began. A triangular frame was developed and new internal substructure inserted to give the ship extra strength. In March 2011, the ship was raised into the air. The modern, supporting frames are grey and the original material is white. Together they ensure Cutty Sark's survival for generations to come.

**REGISTRATION NUMBER**

*In its working life, Cutty Sark had three hatches through which its valuable cargoes were winched in and out. Today, the fore hatch is a staircase and the aft (rear) hatch an access elevator. The main hatch, close to the middle of the deck, was the largest of the three. The top, covered by canvas, can be seen on the Main Deck and the underside is visible on the ship's middle or 'Tween Deck. It is here that the ship's registration number, 63557, is stamped into the iron frame. From 1786, all British ships of more than 15 tons were required to register in their home port. The Mercantile Navy List, detailing all registered ships in Britain and the Empire, was published annually from 1857 until 1976. Cutty Sark is still registered with the same number with the Maritime and Coastguard Agency.*

**THE SHIP'S BELL**

As a working ship, Cutty Sark had two brass bells on the Main Deck – a large one inscribed with the ship's name at the anchor deck and a smaller one to the rear. The bells were used for communication, mainly to mark the passage of time. A day on Cutty Sark was split into five main watches of four hours and two smaller 'dog watches' of two hours, which ensured that sailors followed a different pattern of rest and work each day. Tasks and responsibilities would depend on the ship's progress and a sailor's rank. If there were no sail changes or navigational tasks to deal with, chipping, painting, polishing and repairing would begin. In 1894, apprentice Clarence Ray wrote to his mother: 'Our first job at 5.30 in the morning is to wash the pigs and closets out. I always heard that pigs were unclean animals but now I know it for a positive fact.'

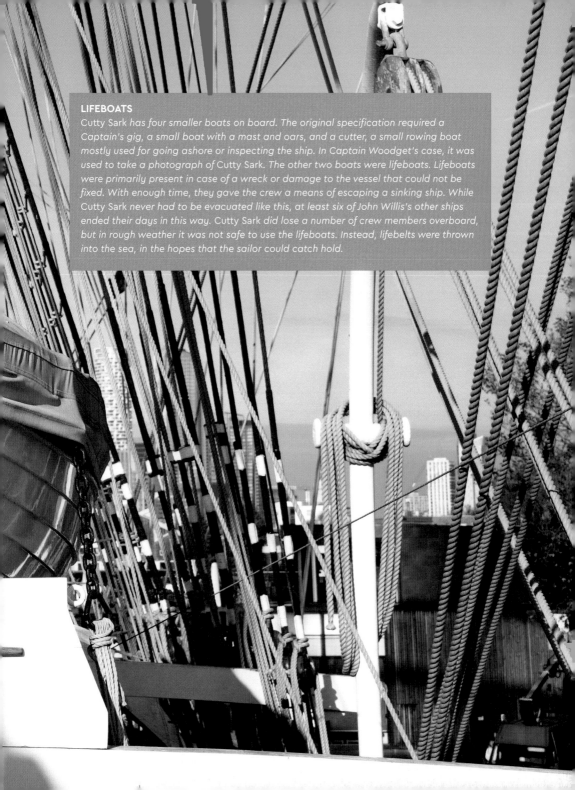

## LIFEBOATS

Cutty Sark *has four smaller boats on board. The original specification required a Captain's gig, a small boat with a mast and oars, and a cutter, a small rowing boat mostly used for going ashore or inspecting the ship. In Captain Woodget's case, it was used to take a photograph of* Cutty Sark. *The other two boats were lifeboats. Lifeboats were primarily present in case of a wreck or damage to the vessel that could not be fixed. With enough time, they gave the crew a means of escaping a sinking ship. While* Cutty Sark *never had to be evacuated like this, at least six of John Willis's other ships ended their days in this way.* Cutty Sark *did lose a number of crew members overboard, but in rough weather it was not safe to use the lifeboats. Instead, lifebelts were thrown into the sea, in the hopes that the sailor could catch hold.*

## THE GALLEY

The galley is the ship's kitchen. The cook had to provide food for the entire crew multiple times per day on different shifts, ensuring everyone received enough to remain healthy and able to do the hard physical labour involved in sailing a ship. With limited supplies that had to last months at sea without refrigeration, this could be a challenge. Using a stove, boiling liquids and keeping a fire burning were all perilous in rough seas. The floor in the galley is covered with ridged tiles to protect the wooden decks from fire and heat, as well as providing grip to prevent people and furniture sliding around in a storm. Sixteen-year-old apprentice Clarence Ray wrote to his mother enthusiastically about food. His favourite was sea pie, an old sailors' recipe, consisting of 'fresh meat and spuds all in soup like, underneath and dough on top'.

## THE FORWARD DECKHOUSE

The forward deckhouse has 12 bunks. At first glance the bunks appear very small. This is not because the crew of Cutty Sark were particularly short but because, if the ship was in heavy seas, rocking and rolling, a snug bunk would help to prevent its occupant falling out. The crew would eat, sleep and rest in its deckhouse. How restful it was would depend on the weather: in 1891, Captain Woodget recorded in his log, 'An immense sea rolled up right aft [...] it dropped on board both sides with tremendous force; smashing in the doors of the fore and after houses [...] the apprentices' house was filled up to the top bunks, soaking everything.' Members of the crew had to bring their own uniform and bedding. Some would arrive well equipped with their possessions kept in a chest or bag and even with a thin mattress known as a donkey's breakfast (as it contained hay). Others, however, had little to bring.

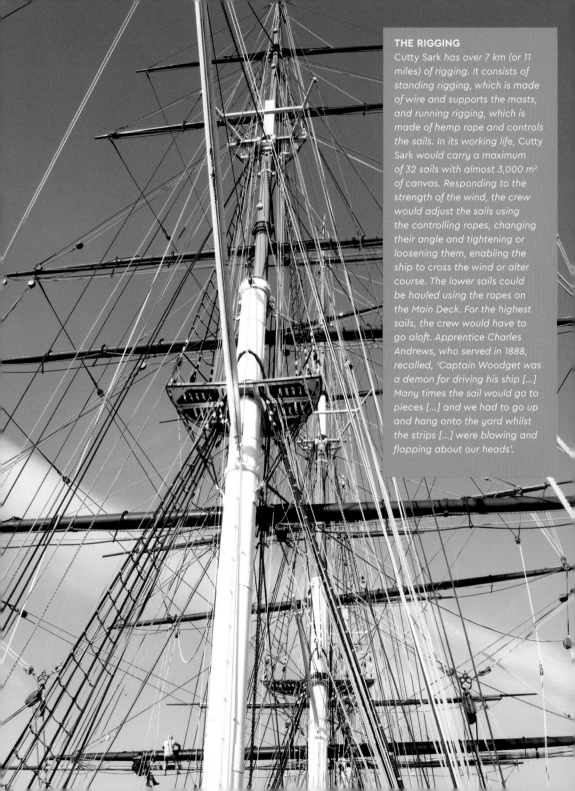

## THE RIGGING

Cutty Sark has over 7 km (or 11 miles) of rigging. It consists of standing rigging, which is made of wire and supports the masts, and running rigging, which is made of hemp rope and controls the sails. In its working life, Cutty Sark would carry a maximum of 32 sails with almost 3,000 m² of canvas. Responding to the strength of the wind, the crew would adjust the sails using the controlling ropes, changing their angle and tightening or loosening them, enabling the ship to cross the wind or alter course. The lower sails could be hauled using the ropes on the Main Deck. For the highest sails, the crew would have to go aloft. Apprentice Charles Andrews, who served in 1888, recalled, 'Captain Woodget was a demon for driving his ship [...] Many times the sail would go to pieces [...] and we had to go up and hang onto the yard whilst the strips [...] were blowing and flapping about our heads'.

## THE MASTER'S SALOON

The master's saloon on Cutty Sark is the most luxurious area of the ship. It is French polished and decorated with teak and birdseye maple panelling and gilded corbels. The officers of the ship (master, first mate, steward) would eat in this area and, once in port, the captain entertained here. The circular dishes that hang from the ceiling above the table are known as gimbles. With slots for drinks to sit safely, they were an ingenious way of preventing spillages if the ship was rocking. The officers had their own cabins, adjacent to the saloon. The ship's accommodation was organised according to hierarchy. The least qualified on board, the ordinary and able seamen, slept in the forward deckhouse, towards the bow of the ship. The petty officers (carpenter, sailmaker, cook) and apprentices slept in the aft deckhouse, towards the stern (back) of the ship, with the officers at the very rear.

## FIGUREHEADS

Figureheads are carved sculptures that decorate the bows of sailing ships. Such ships were subject to perilous conditions and figureheads often became an emblem of the vessel, a protector of the ship and its crew. The subjects are wide-ranging, from shipowners' family members to contemporary politicians like William Ewart Gladstone and William Wilberforce, or famed individuals like Florence Nightingale to figures from literature or folklore like Lalla Rookh or Nannie herself. The inspiration behind some is entirely unknown and they were likely salvaged from wrecks. Cutty Sark now holds the world's largest collection of figureheads from merchant ships. These figureheads were originally donated in the 1950s by Sydney Cumbers (1875–1959), also known as 'Long John Silver' due to the distinctive eye patch he wore. He had a passion for maritime artefacts, and a vast collection, including 82 figureheads, which was displayed at The Look-Out in Gravesend, before being donated to Cutty Sark in 1953.

## Explore more at Royal Museums Greenwich

There's plenty more to see and do at Royal Museums Greenwich. Our Museums are all within easy walking distance of each other and together they offer a culture-filled, fun day out for all ages.

## Learning at *Cutty Sark*

Enjoy an annual programme of events and activities that celebrates and investigates the ship's history. From Sea Shanty festivals to scrimshaw workshops, you'll find something for everyone on board *Cutty Sark*.

## Support

The valuable support of our Members, Patrons, donors and sponsors allows us to continue our important work through exhibitions, loans, conferences, publications, learning programmes and community initiatives. Please give generously to help us continue this vital work. You can donate at donate.rmg.co.uk. Alternatively, you can donate by credit card by calling the Individual Giving team on +(44) 20 8312 6603, or leave a donation next time you visit. Our donation boxes are located in and around the Museum galleries. Every pound makes a difference.

## Membership

If you've enjoyed your day in Greenwich, why not consider becoming a Member? Enjoy unlimited entry to our four unique attractions: *Cutty Sark*, the Royal Observatory, National Maritime Museum and the Queen's House all year, including free entry to special exhibitions. Membership also includes invitations to private views, special Members' events, discounts in the shop, café and on public events as well as access to a lovely Members' Room and a biannual Members' magazine. Members may also purchase an annual guest pass at the Admission desk or from the Membership office. There's really no better way to enjoy the adventure. Visit rmg.co.uk/membership for more information.